Trinity Equestrian Center...

"Trinity Equestrian Center is a beautiful 67-acre horse lover's paradise located on the shores of Cooley Lake just 4 miles south of Eau Claire on Hwy 37. Bill & Toni Mattson and Jan Behm have owned Trinity since 2002.

As owners, we consider ourselves so very blessed and love using our horses and center to inspire the lives of ALL people, but have a particular heart to serve the at-risk and underprivileged.

Our philosophy and activities are Christian-based and rooted in our belief that the blessings we receive are to be shared with others to become blessings to them as well.

We are a 501(c)3 non-profit organization. All proceeds from our full service horse center offering boarding, training, lessons, therapeutic riding, horse leasing, day camps and Ranch Care (summer care program) go to fund our mission of connecting people, horses and God."

(www.trinity-ec.com)

Perhaps I should begin by introducing myself. My name is Mike. Mike Switzer. My friend is Nathan Haynes (hereafter referred to as 'the talent'.). He's a professional photographer in the UK (and if you've ever been to a Western horse show over there you've probably seen him. He's a mixture of tattoos, a camera, and the need to keep whistling and throwing things to get the horses ears to go forward.)

Nathan and his family recently visited us here in Eau Claire, Wisconsin - And that visit ultimately ended in the book you are holding. But first, let me step back several years to give you some background to our story...

I met my wife at school. We were both fourteen at the time... She had just arrived from the USA and was this startling, glamorous, beautiful new stranger. I couldn't tear my eyes off her - But never took things any further as I wasn't sure she was interested in me, (even when she started sitting on my lap in drama class... What can I say? Like a fine wine - I was slow to mature).

The unfortunate truth behind this story is that Elizabeth's Father passed away suddenly in 1985, and her Mom (who was from England) relocated them both shortly thereafter. Elizabeth felt scared, and alone, and a long way from home.

Many years passed after school, and for several of them we never saw each other - then we reconnected and, ultimately, married. As I write this, we've had eighteen wonderful years of marriage. In that time, there is one thing I've grown to know about my wife - one thing that runs through every vein of her being - and that is her loyalty. She has a fierce pride - and nowhere is that more obvious than in her patriotism. She has always been a proud American - and she has longed to return home for many, many years.

Actually, 'longing' isn't the right word. It's not strong enough... Nor is 'pining'. She *ached* to be back home...

Where other people have a sense of comfort and familiarity, Liz had a void. It killed me that I was unable to restore that part of her.

Every night she would go to sleep and dream of the fourth of July... and Thanksgiving... and Stars & Stripes... and Eagles.

"From the oyster to the eagle, from the swine to the tiger, all animals are to be found in men and each of them exists in some man, sometimes several at the time. Animals are nothing but the portrayal of our virtues and vices made manifest to our eyes, the visible reflections of our souls. God displays them to us to give us food for thought."

Victor Hugo

Finally, in 2008, when the opportunity presented itself, we decided to uproot the family and take a leap of faith.

Full disclosure time: I have never been particularly religious - although always spiritual. In my case, there is a certain amount of fear - How do I accept that there's something so *huge*, so *unknowable*, and so *different*? How could *that* God care about something as minor as me?

When we came to make such a life-altering decision, I decided to put aside those fears, and doubts, and hesitation - and pray for good fortune instead.

...And as the process started, we found that things began to click into place. We sold our house at the right time - Our immigration went through at just the right time - We found the perfect place to move to in Eau Claire, Wisconsin...

...And that brings us back to Trinity Equestrian Center. We shipped our horses over to Trinity in December 2007 - in preparation for our arrival the following March. Elizabeth has always been extremely close to her horses - and it takes a great deal of trust for her to relinquish control to someone else. As part of her research of the area, she happened upon Trinity Equestrian Center. She had many email and phone conversations with the owners, in order to ensure that everything was fine. We were pleased to discover that, in addition to being wonderfully warm people, they also applied their faith to allow them to give something back to the local community.

Trinity offers Ranch Care which is their Christian based summer camp for 7-12 year olds. It offers outdoor sports and riding and field trips and fun! But they also offer 'healing with horses' (a therapeutic riding program), equine assisted psychotherapy, and many other programs for the at-risk and underprivileged. It was a little humbling when we first arrived - but then exciting as we began to realize that God finds a way to care for everyone and everything - no matter their place in the Universe.

It was on one of our first visits that I stood outside with Elizabeth and watched the sun set on another beautiful day. She turned to me and thanked me for bringing her home. She said she finally felt at peace. I agreed - and as we looked out into the horizon we could see an Eagle watching over us in the distance...

Nathan & Tracy came to visit us after our first year in Eau Claire. We had spent the last twelve months telling everyone how wonderful it was - and begging people to come stay. Of course, now they had finally called our bluff. Suddenly we were concerned that the things we had found beautiful - they'd find tacky. We prayed that we could have the opportunity to show them something memorable - so that they could take a little part of our lives back home with them.

On their first day, we took them to visit at Trinity. Nathan immediately saw the beauty and serenity of everything around us. He began to take pictures of anything and everything. In only a year, I'd begun to lose sight of the beauty that surrounds this place - even when it was staring me in the face every day.

We walked to the other end of the barn, and I found Elizabeth with Molly (her horse). I could see the other horses being fed in the field. It was then that the truth of Trinity's quote ("Connecting People, Horses & God"), struck me.

A horse-lover has a connection with their horse that cannot be matched by any other animal. A dog is a companion - A horse will give you a place in their herd.

"There is something about the outside of a horse that is good for the inside of a man."
Winston Churchill

"A man on a horse is spiritually as well as physically bigger than a man on foot."
John Steinbeck

"The horse is God's gift to mankind."
Arabian Proverb

"In my opinion, a horse is the animal to have. Eleven-hundred pounds of raw muscle, power, grace and sweat between your legs - it's something you just can't get from a pet hamster."
Author Unknown

We concluded our visit with the horses and began to make our way down to the lake. Nathan was thrilled with the photographic opportunities he had been presented with. But I, being not only less talented, but of much weaker character, still wanted something exceptional to finish out the day.

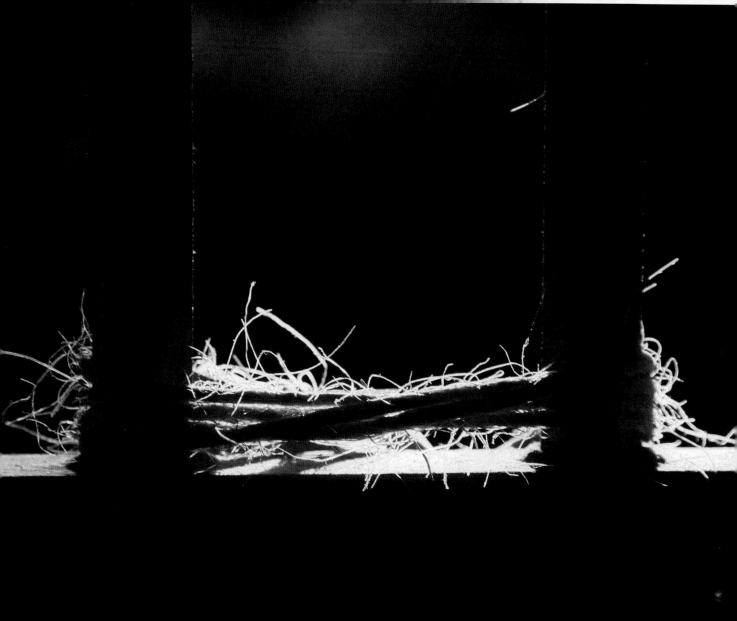

"When despair for the world grows in me,
and I wake in the night at the least sound.
In fear of what my life and my children's
lives may be. I go and lie down where the
wood drake rests in his beauty on the water,
and the great heron feeds. I come into the
peace of wild things who do not tax their
lives with forethought or grief.
I come into the presence of still water.
And I feel above me the day blind stars
waiting with their light.
For a time I rest in the grace of the world
and am free"

(Wendell Berry)

We continue around the lake - and as I saw the full beauty of nature in front of me, I realize the lesson that I had been too blind to see until that very moment.

It's easy to let life pass us by.

...To let the good things go unnoticed as we concentrate on the bad.

It's too easy to work toward some 'someday' that never comes, without noticing the day that is already here.

I had been praying for something special to show Nathan. While I had prayed, Nathan had the vision to *enjoy* the minor things... To appreciate the simple things. And, in doing so, he made them magnificent.

Before we moved, I was concerned that God wouldn't want my faith, as I hadn't visited his house in many years. Then, when we first arrived in the USA (and at Trinity), I had seen an Eagle watching us from afar. What I didn't understand until now was that God wasn't concerned that I didn't visit his house = he'd been watching over us throughout. All things that had happened in our lives were small steps to getting us there - at that very point, on that very day. Every new thing from this point on should be an experience, and we should learn new lessons as we each make our way through our own personal adventure.

I finally stopped trying to impress Nathan. Instead, I let him show me the things that had passed me by for the last twelve months.

"One reason why birds and horses are happy is because they are not trying to impress other birds and horses."
(Dale Carnegie)

"One hour of life, crowded to the full
with glorious action, and filled with
noble risks, is worth whole years of
those mean observances of paltry
decorum, in which men steal
through
existence, like sluggish waters
through
a marsh, without either honor or
observation."
(Sir Walter Scott)

"The blessings we receive are to be shared with others to become blessings to them as well."
(Trinity Equestrian Center)

And so our day drew to a close. I thanked the sky one more time for a beautiful day. Nathan and I discussed putting some of the pictures he had taken into a book, so that others could appreciate the wonderful location that is Trinity. In every nook and cranny you will find some fascination, some interest - or just someone making something *better*. It is both inspiring and awesome - and I hope you get to visit one day and experience it for yourself.

As for me - I guess on one level God is unknowable. But equally - I've seen his hands now. They are the hands of the people all over the world that spread his word and do good work. His eyes are those people that take action when they see an injustice. And his voice is the sound of nature itself.

Nathan and I walked back to the car...

God is all around us. And sometimes he teaches a lesson.

...And sometimes, when we've learned that lesson - He just wants to remind us that he's there.

"The Eagle, he was Lord above."
(William Wordsworth)